16 Easy Tips To Restoring Your Relationship

Get your Ex Back With These Easy Steps

Written by

Donna Lewis

"Don't worry about losing. If it is right, it happens - The Main thing is not to hurry. Nothing good gets away."

~John Steinbeck

Contents

16 Easy Tips to Restoring Your Relationship

Don't beg and plead for a second chance just right after the break up

If the break up is still fresh it would be best if you won't go begging and pleading for a second chance. Yes, this might work but it won't really do your relationship any good. Why? Because your partner may give you a second chance but not because your partner really wants it, instead your partner will somehow feel pressured or guilty to see you on your knees begging. That is definitely not a good start for a second chance. It might lead to resentment or any negative emotion that might blow your relationship to a final end at the first rise of conflict.

Sure you just want to express your feelings to your partner. You want them to know that you really care for them and you want your relationship to work. However, your partner won't ask for break up for no reason - if your ex wants a space from your relationship it only means he/she wants a space – maybe your partner needs some time to think things over or your ex needs some time alone. If your partner still loves you and still wants to be with you they'll tell you. So you just don't have to rush things up. Give your partner some space for awhile. Let your partner think, and it would also be best if you'll also think things over.

Give your selves some time to miss each other. Give your ex and yourself space so your ex will have room to miss you. Allow yourself to have a cooling off period. Maybe you can temporarily stop seeing each other for awhile. Set a specific time to see your ex again. Like after one month. Do all your best to never do something to see your ex before your specified date. Yes, you'll be thinking about him or her, but you can't allow your feelings to override the break that you both need.

If you really want to get back with your ex, you need time to clear your head and become rational again. Then you'll be able to see where things truly fell apart. You'll also be able to open real lines of communication when there's a little time and distance between the two of you.

Being reunited after is surely sweeter.

Be patient and accept that it takes time to get your ex back

Try to be cool and relaxed. Again, never try to hurry things up. Don't rush things, as you will look only desperate, this is a very important thing to do. You should understand that this is a very delicate situation, both of you are emotionally hurt, what is important, is that you are careful in handling the situation or you might end up doing worse.

First of all, analyze your break-up. There should be a very good reason why you guys broke up. Try to think and analyze, once you found the reason. Study it, know how can you deal with it, how can you fix it, how can you show your ex that you are now a changed person, that things now are better.

If the break-up was your entire fault, have the initiative to contact your ex and recognize your mistake. Be humble – accept your mistakes and move on. Show your ex that you are sorry for what you have done, show genuine effort.

Surely she/he will appreciate it. Let them know that you are sorry for your actions and you accepted and respected their decision, Show him/her that you are responsible enough and ready for a second chance. Instead of focusing on your feelings of rejection, loneliness, and hurt give yourself some time away from your ex to straighten your mind up and rational. Eventually allow you to accomplish what you really want in the end – reconciliation.

Be happy!

Or at least try to be happy, smile. Show the people that you are okay, that you have moved on. Let your ex know that you were sorry yet try not to look so bad. It will make your ex appreciate the positivity within you and make them see you have become more matured with the situation. If they see positive side of you they will see how lucky they are to have you and will definitely welcome you back to their lives.

Being sad and gloomy will really not help you, it will just cause you to lose your self-esteem and confidence. Thus, it will only make things worst for you. When you are sad you won't be able to think straight, which might make you do some things that will just add up to your sadness. You are in a very down situation, I know, and being happy might be the hardest thing to do. Yet, letting your sadness succumb you is not the best situation to be in if you want to get your ex back.

Give your self some time during the break up. This is the best time to focus on your self. Give your self a chance to be alone. To do things on your own: to do shopping alone, jog alone or drink your favorite cup of coffee alone. Why? These things will let you remember you are an individual and can still be happy just being with your self. Love your self back – sometimes when we love someone we become selfless it is just high time to focus on your self again and love your self more. Then, happiness will come by being alone.

When your ex sees you are happy and positive he/she will surely start thinking and assess things and will definitely consider a second chance with you.

Avoid depression

It's very normal for you to feel sad and depressed after a breakup. But it's important that you don't end up so depressed you don't want to live anymore or fall into a pit of despair. That is if you really want and working toward getting back with your ex. Try to avoid some things that will make you think more about the break up that might drown you more to sadness and depression.

One way to keep away from depression is to socialize. Go out and have a good time. Meet new friends and do new things. You can even go out on a date again. If someone asks you on a date then go out. Often times, when your ex see's you are dating another person he/she might get jealous and will let them feel the need to get you back.

If your ex sees you are fine this will show them that you are not going to let things get you down, you are showing that you are strong enough to move on and push on forward. A quality that is very attractive to many.

Think of the reasons why you broke up

Lovers don't leave or ask for a break for no reason. They just can't go hurting themselves suffering and going through heartache and the pain of breaking apart for nothing.

If you are trying to get an ex back the knowing and thinking of the real reason that caused the break up would be the best thing to do. Know why they left or asked for a break and think of the things that contributed to it. Pinpoint the reasons why you think you broke up so you'll know where and what to change in case you are back with your ex to avoid breaking up again.

If you already know the real reasons that contributed to the break up, think of ways to improve your self. Like, if your partner left you because he/she found unappreciated anymore then you might want to improve on that first. Try to think of some simple ways that your ex did to you and appreciate it even if he or she can't hear your words of appreciation anymore it would still help if you get use to it. Then if you are back in each others arm, appreciating words will come out naturally from you.

Or if your partner broke up with you because they found you nagging to death then it would be high time to start changing. Try to instill in your mind that nagging won't do any good in your relationship so if you are back in each other's lives it won't cause another break up.

Knowing why your relationship ended is the best way to start working to bring back your estranged partner. Know why and work on the reasons why you broke up.

Learn from the situation
and accept

In a relationship, there are two persons, so if it breaks apart the blame should be on both of you. In every action there is always an equivalent reaction. Take time to figure out everything, and you will find out, that you both had something to do with the break-up, not just your ex or not just you.

Maybe you didn't have the same interests. Maybe your family or religious beliefs were different. It's possible that you just didn't have much fun together or you didn't have much to talk about.

Well, that's a fact. Two people can't be similar in everything. Every one is different. We have our own flaws and strengths. If we love someone we should learn to accept everything about him/her including the differences of your individuality.

If your relationship ended because of these differences then I think the best way to go is to learn to accept your partner - everything about your partner. And then from acceptance go for realization of your mistakes and then learn from it. Spend some time evaluating what it is that went wrong. Then make sure that as you seek out new relationships or if you are back with each other you don't make the same mistakes.

Fix the broken or what ever that need fixing

Something contributed to the break up. Maybe you did something wrong or your partner did something wrong. Break ups happen because one inflicted pain to the other or caused unhappiness. In short, break ups happen for a reason.

If your relationship was broken and you want to bring back the lost love then sure there's a need for fixing. Fix whatever needs fixing.

Start with yourself. Fix your self first. Accept the things that came along with your break up. Accept the pain, sadness, loneliness, guilt or whatever emotions that stirred within you after the break up. Deal with it and make yourself better. Work on healing your self first. Think of the reasons why you broke up and work on it to do better.

If you are sure you have already fixed yourself then it's time to start fixing your relationship.

Try to be friends with your
ex - just a friend

Yes, you can show your love even if you're just friends, be casual, show friendly support and let them feel that you are still there for them. Show your care and love in a friendly way. Try your best to limit the contact but keep yourself open and be ready anytime; you don't know when your ex might need your help. However, make sure that your actions will not be judged or misunderstood by your ex as a desperate move to get her/him back – offer pure friendship. Friendship will build trust between the both of you and will help you get close again.

Finally, when the right time comes, try to ask them, why they broke up with you, but be casual about it rather than appear desperate. Have an open conversation with your ex so he/she will open up and tell you what he/she was thinking when you broke up. Hopefully, after a good friendly conversation, you'll know the reason why you broke up, which will help you evaluate your feelings and know what points to deal and strategies to do to win your ex back. After a good talk things will be better for the both of you. You can use the information to help get him back and to learn to not commit the same mistakes you did before.

Look good everyday and work on improving your self

Always be at your best look – impress yourself and your ex physically, this will help you raise your self-esteem and confidence. Be confident and always have a positive attitude towards everything, this will help you react to things better. Rather than going around gloomy and lonely, try to be happy with your friends or new friends. This will help you improve yourself.

Do not to let your appearance suffer because of a break up. This is a big sign that you are getting hit really badly by it. Maintain a good appearance. Do not let your appearance reflect your situation; get your hair done, work-out, etc. Do not stop looking good because you are hurting. Take care of yourself. Yes, looks can help. Your ex might want you again with your looks and attractiveness. You will definitely not be very attractive to your ex if you stop fixing yourself. You must remember to be at your best look at all times if you are on your way to get your ex back.

Also work on improving yourself. Don't get so down because of the break up. Continue working on your improvement, change is not immediate and takes time. Keep working on what ever you need to. It will pay off in the long run.

Bring back the person that your ex fell in love with

Think of the things that made your ex fell in love with you. I believe at the beginning of your relationship with your ex you were showered with sweet words and appreciation. Work on these things that made your ex appreciate you. This is important to know because this is where you'll start in your quest to bring your ex back.

Start by thinking of the things that attracted your ex the first day you met. Was it your eyes? Was it your sexy body or your smile? Identify what attracted him/her to you and work on making them attracted to him again.

Also think of the things that you liked doing together. Did you like to travel on the first stage of your relationship? Did you like to picnic and share romantic moments under the moonlight? Think of the things that you might do in case you are given the chance to get back to your ex.

Remember everything you did that built your relationship. You need to get back to it in order to reunite and to keep your ex forever. Think back of the things that made you fell in love to each other then work on it to rekindle the love and to keep the flame glowing.

Make the first move

After making yourself confident and assured, you can start getting your ex back by trying to communicate. Listen, you have limited your communication with each other. There is no way, that your ex has not missed you. Maybe, at this time your ex might be dying to hear from you.

Now is the time to communicate with your ex and make the first move. Try to call or e-mail, text your ex, and invite him/her somewhere, so you can talk, might as well be just coffee in the café.

Do not make them feel like you are trying to get them to talk about your relationship, the purpose of this, is to show to your ex that you are still his/her friend.

Be casual; tell them, that you just want to catch up with each other, that you guys will go out as friends. It is very advisable not to invite them for dinner or something because it will appear like you are trying to invite them for a date. Just appear calm and cool, if they say no, then you can accept them and leaving them with the "oh okay, next time".

Doing this will make your ex appreciate you even more, and if friendly date becomes successful, it might lead to your knowing, whether your ex is still interested in you.

Hope for the best - but do not expect

After your date, specifically your friendly date, you might have assessed if you both were happy during the date. You might have gone to the movies or somewhere else.

You might have felt the reconnection of the sparks. But you need to be very careful with your assessment; this might be just because you missed each other.

After the date, all you have to do is to wait for signals for another date, or maybe a romantic date. Just hope for the best, do not assume that you have won and you are getting your ex back. It is better to stay on the safe side so you don't get disappointed and end up being broken-hearted again if it will end not the way you wanted it to.

If you feel like your ex is showing a little bit of interest in you or you feel like she is starting to flirt with you again, or spends time with you again, then it is okay to be hopeful, but don't expect, just hope for the best!

You might be noticing signs that your ex is interested in getting you back, that's okay, you are right, but as I have said you shouldn't jump into things, because if things go wrong, you might get hurt. It is always better to be on the safe side.

Play hard to get

The best way to get your ex back is to play hard to get, because if you push yourself, you might actually be pushing your ex farther away from you.

By nature, man yearns to have what is not theirs. To simply put, if you play hard to get you might build an interest to your partner. Knowing that you have somehow managed to move on and not so in to your ex anymore would make your ex more interested in you.

Another advantage of playing hard to get is that: you can assess the reaction of your ex - if your ex is showing interest on you again. Control yourselves guys, yes, I know, you are missing your ex, but think also, that they also miss you. It just natural on relationships that lasted long, like years, that you guys will miss each other – happy memories and etc. So be in Control, and don't dive in. Pretend hard to get even if you are dying to have him back again inside. Build a renewed interest and let that interest blossom until your ex realizes he/she wants and needs you back.

Evaluation of your feelings
after reconnection

Getting better eh? You both might be going out often now. You both might be in the comfort zone of each other now. You think you are almost there.

Before assuming and working that, we need to think first if you are doing the right thing. Try to think on what's going to happen in the long run. Ask yourself, If you both will continue being excited on seeing each other – probably not.

Be more rational, don't jump into conclusions. Now is the time to re-evaluate your feelings. Remember that, you both are just going out as friends maybe best friends. Surely, that will change if you get into a commitment. Try to consider all the factors that will be affected if you are going to pursue.

Keeping the Fun alive

The dates worked right? Why not continue doing them. Movies and dinners are always romantic, but you would not want to do them always as it will become stale and boring. Try to use your imagination and creativity and plan for more fun activities. This will make your partner appreciate you even more – and of course, love you more.

You guys can try:

•   Going to the beach

•   Watch movies together in house, or cinemas

•   Going camping

•   Swimming

•   Biking together

•   Golfing, ice skating, canoeing

•   Playing cards

•   Vacation with the family

- Travel together

- Doing things your partner always wanted

- Learning new things together through classes: dancing, singing, etc

- Picnic

Try to use your imagination and create more fun dates. You can always ask suggestion from your partner. Giving your relationship variety of things to do will maintain the spark. Do not be afraid of trying new things, it is through experience you will learn how to deal with things.

Be more romantic with your ex everyday. Give yourself time to focus on them everyday, to check on how they are doing. You can leave them cute notes expressing your love. Giving them single flowers, kissing and hugging them will make them feel your presence. Learn things on your own. All these things will depend on you and how your partner reacts on certain things, be serious and exert effort; surely you will be much appreciated by your partner.

Go on with your life

Whether you are positive you can win your ex back or not remember to think of your self and put your self first. Don't try to focus all of your attention to your ex and how you can get him/her back. Although you desperately want your ex back do not lose the love for your self. Be in control. Try to continue living a normal life. So if you fail in winning your ex back at least you still have your self and starting over again without your ex will not be too difficult anymore.

If, fortunately, everything you did paid off – you are back in your ex's arms again remember to learn from your mistakes. Don't go around repeating your mistakes, learn from them. And apply what you have learned. Show your ex that you have learned your lesson and that you can both go on with your life happily.

www.ingramcontent.com/pod-product-compliance
Lightning Source LLC
Chambersburg PA
CBHW071253280526
45788CB00004B/1698